NATIONAL GEOGRAPHIC CHANNEL

# GREAT
# MIGRATIONS

# Amazing Animal
# Journeys

## Laura Marsh

NATIONAL
GEOGRAPHIC

Washington, D.C.

: Claire, Kendall, Ingrid, and Catherine  — L.F.M.

**Library of Congress Cataloging-in-Publication Data**
Marsh, Laura F.
Great migrations. Amazing animal journeys / by Laura Marsh.
p. cm.
Includes index.
ISBN 978-1-4263-0741-6 (pbk. : alk. paper) -- ISBN 978-1-4263-0742-3 (library binding : alk. paper)
1. Animal migration--Juvenile literature. I. Title.
QL754.M27 2010
591.56'8--dc22

2010017958

Abbreviation Key: GET = Getty Images; IS = iStockphoto.com; NGS = NationalGeographicStock.com; NGT = National Geographic Television

cover, Paul Nicklen/ NGS; 1, John Hicks/ NGS; 2, Selyutina Olga/ Shutterstock; 4, Paul Nicklen/ NGS; 5 (top), Mike Powels/ Oxford Scientific/ Photolibrary; 5 (bottom), NGT; 6-7, Ruud de Man/ IS; 7 (inset), Eric Isselée/ IS; 8, Beverly Joubert/ NGS; 10-11, Pete Oxford/ naturepl.com; 11 (bottom), Karine Aigner; 12-13, NGT; 13 (top), Beverly Joubert/ NGS; 14, NGT; 15, Volkmar K. Wentzel/ NGS;16-17, Richard Du Toit/ Minden Pictures/ NGS; 18-19, NGT; 19 (inset), Mlenny Photograhy/ Alexander Hafemann/ IS; 20, John Hicks/ NGS; 22 (top), John Hicks/ NGS; 22 (bottom), Hugh Yorkston/ NGS; 23 (top), NGT; 23 (bottom), NGT; 24 (top), NGT; 24 (bottom), NGT; 25 (top left), NGT; 25 (top right), Mlenny Photograhy/ Alexander Hafemann/ IS; 25 (bottom), NGT; 26 (top), Roger Garwood/ NGS; 26 (center), NGT; 26 (bottom), NGT; 27, Roger Garwood/ NGS; 28, Roger Garwood/ NGS; 29, Stephen Belcher/ Minden Pictures; 30-31, Jo Overholt / AlaskaStock.com; 31 (inset), Flip Nicklen/ Minden Pictures/ /NGS;32 (inset), Flip Nicklen/ Minden Pictures/ NGS; 32, NGT; 33, Stock Connection/ Fotosearch; 34, NGT; 36, Paul Nicklen/ NGS; 37 (top), Paul Nicklen/ NGS; 37 (bottom), Paul Nicklen/ NGS; 38 (top), Paul Nicklen/ NGS; 38 (center), Bob Halstead/ Lonely Planet Images/ GET; 38 (bottom), Alex Potemkin/ IS; 39, Paul Nicklen/ NGS; 40-41, Norbert Rosing/ NGS; 41 (inset), Flip Nicklen/ Minden Pictures/ NGS; 42, Michio Hoshino/ Minden Pictures/ NGS; 43, Ricardo Savi/ The Image Bank/ GET; 44, Myrleen Pearson/ Alamy; 45, Ralph Lee Hopkins/ NGS; 46 (top right), NGT; 46 (center left), Mike Powles/ Oxford Scientific/ Photolibrary; 46

Printed in China
10/RRDS/1

# Table of Contents

# On the Move

When animals travel from one region or climate to another, it is called migration. Animals migrate in search of food or a mate. Migration helps animals survive on Earth.

Many animals migrate. This book is about zebras, red crabs, and walruses. Their great migrations are incredible journeys.

Walrus

Zebra

Red Crab

## Word Wise

MIGRATION: Moving from one region or habitat to another for food or a mate

MATE: Either a male or female in a pair. Most animals need a mate to have babies.

# Zebras

**LIFE SPAN:** Average 25 years

**SIZE:** Up to 60 inches tall at shoulder

**WEIGHT:** 440–990 pounds. That's about 3 to 6 adult men put together!

**COAT:** Shiny, eliminates 70 percent of heat

**TAIL:** Tufted at tip, unlike a horse's tail

**LEGS:** Can run 35–40 miles an hour

**HOOVES:** Protect feet over rough terrain. Powerful kick fights off predators.

**MANE:** Hair sticks up and is striped, unlike a horse's mane

**MOUTH:** Eats mostly grasses and roots

**TEETH:** Delivers a painful bite used for protection

**STRIPES:** Act as camouflage to break up outline of zebra's body

## Survival Stripes

Every zebra has a different stripe pattern—like a human fingerprint. A newborn zebra learns its mother's pattern right away so it can identify her.

Word Wise

CAMOUFLAGE: An animal's natural color or form that allows it to blend in with its surroundings

In Botswana, Africa, up to 30,000 zebras migrate every year. Thousands of zebras travel in herds and live in the Makgadikgadi (MAH-kgah-dee-kgah-dee) and Nxai (NIGH) Pan National Park.

Scientists believe their journey is about 360 miles round-trip. That's like walking across the state of Wyoming!

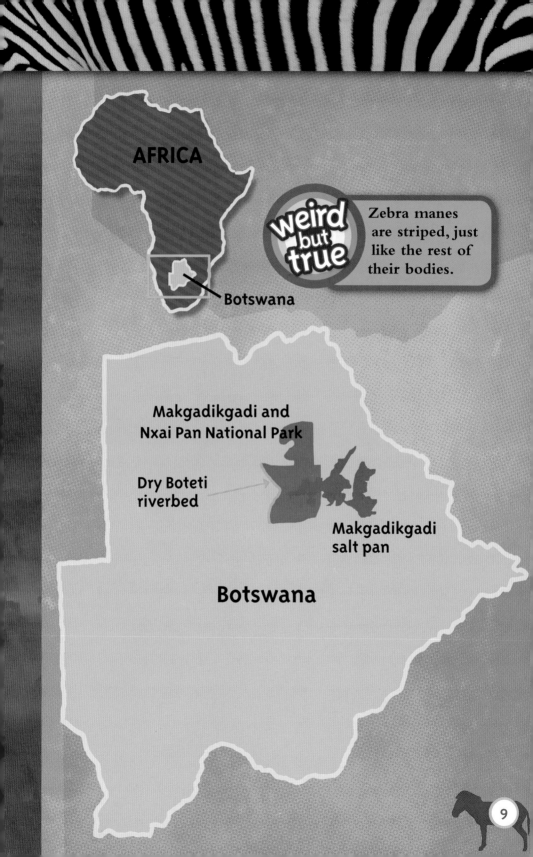

AFRICA

Botswana

**weird but true**

Zebra manes are striped, just like the rest of their bodies.

Makgadikgadi and Nxai Pan National Park

Dry Boteti riverbed

Makgadikgadi salt pan

Botswana

During the dry season, the zebras stay near the Boteti River. It is the only water source available. All other water holes dry up. Around the river basin, zebras eat grasses and roots.

After several months, most of the nutritious food is gone. So when the rainy season begins, the zebras move east to the flooded Makgadikgadi salt pans.

New grasses and new water holes spring up with the rains there. The zebras stay five to eight months, until the water holes dry up. Then they return to the Boteti River basin.

# Water Emergency

In recent years, cattle owned by local people were drinking the water and eating the grasses along the Boteti River area. But there was a problem. There was not enough food and water for all of the cattle and wild animals. Zebras were getting pushed out. They had to find water holes farther away from the Boteti River.

Zebras in other parts of Africa usually travel less than ten miles from their water source to find food. But in the Makgadikgadi, zebras had to travel as many as 21 miles. Sometimes zebras went without water for a whole week. Many

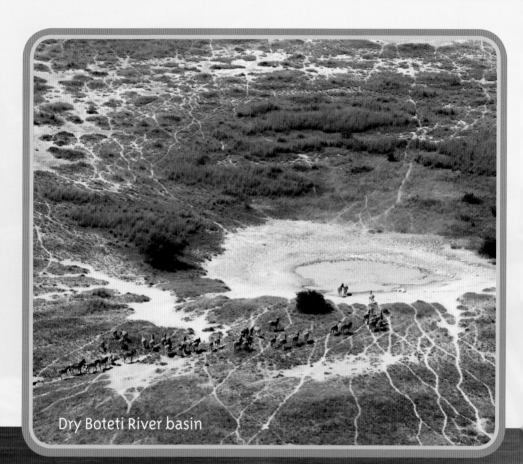

Dry Boteti River basin

Zebras can move their large ears without moving their body. This lets them find and identify a sound without attracting attention.

People decided to do something about the problem. In 2004, a large fence was placed in the Makgadikgadi and Nxai Pan National Park. Now the 150-mile fence separates the cattle and zebras so they each have their own territory.

Also, man-made water holes with pumps were added around the Boteti River basin.

weird but true

Zebra skin is black. White fur makes the white stripes. Even under the white stripes, the skin is black.

15

**Q** If a dictionary goes from A to Z, what goes from Z to A?

**A** Zebra

Scientists are studying the zebras and their babies, hoping that their numbers will grow. They want the zebras to be healthy for many years to come.

# Red Crabs

**LIFE SPAN:** About 12 years

**SIZE:** Up to four and a half inches across

**WEIGHT:** One pound

**LEGS:** Used to walk. Have eight legs, four on each side.

**FRONT CLAWS:** Used to put food in their mouths

**MOUTH:** Eats fruit, seeds, leaves, flowers, dead birds, and even other dead crabs. They are scavengers.

**GILLS & LUNGS:** Used to breathe air. Adult crabs cannot breathe underwater.

**Word Wise**

**SCAVENGER:** An animal that feeds on dead plants and animals and items left behind by others

**weird but true**

Crabs use almost the exact same migration route every year.

On Christmas Island off the coast of Australia, up to 120 million red crabs migrate from the forest floor to the ocean every year. It is a long five-mile journey full of danger.

The red crab's body is built for life on land. But their young can only hatch in ocean water. So the crabs migrate to find a mate and release their eggs in the ocean.

**1 Red crabs leave their forest homes.**

Red crabs come out of their holes, called burrows, after the season's first big rain. They travel from their forest home for more than one week. They cross roads and climb down 40-foot cliffs. Finally, they reach the ocean.

**2 Millions of crabs must climb down steep ciffs to reach the ocean.**

Male crabs get there first to dig burrows. Then the females arrive and the males fertilize the eggs inside the female's bodies. Males return to the forest while the females stay in the burrows for up to 13 days.

**4** Females leave the burrow after almost two weeks.

Before dawn, the female crabs leave their burrows, enter the water, and perform a kind of dance to release their eggs into the ocean. A female can release up to 100,000 eggs! Then they return to the forest.

Word Wise

LARVAE: An animal's wormlike form that hatches from an egg

INSTINCT: Behavior that animals are born knowing how to do

The eggs hatch into larvae in the ocean. After three to four weeks, the larvae change into young crabs and crawl up on land. The tiny crabs are about a quarter of an inch long.

## Pink Tide

When the baby crabs leave the ocean and walk toward the forest, they look like a pink tide. The babies know how to get to the forest by instinct.

25

# Danger!

The red crabs face many dangers during their migration. Cars and other vehicles drive over them. Many drown in waves and the larvae get eaten by fish. Yellow crazy ants attack them. Some crabs get too hot in the sun and dry out.

vehicles

waves

yellow crazy ants

# Helping Red Crabs

People are working to keep red crabs safe during their migration. Walls and tunnels have been built to funnel crabs under roadways, so fewer crabs get run over by cars. Some roads are even closed during the migration.

ROAD CLOSED
RED CRAB MIGRATION
NO ENTRY BY VEHICLES
BEYOND THIS POINT

**weird but true**

Crabs live in a forest burrow all year when not migrating. Only one crab lives in each burrow.

29

# Walruses

**LIFE SPAN:** Up to 40 years

**SIZE:** Up to 12 feet long

**WEIGHT:** Up to 3,400 pounds

**SKIN:** Appears brown or gray in the water. Pink or dark brown when not in the water.

**FLIPPERS:** Rear flippers used to swim and move on land

**BLUBBER:** Can be two to four and a half inches thick. Insulates body from cold air and water.

**AIR POUCH:** Can be inflated to keep head above water while sleeping

**Word Wise**

BLUBBER: Fat surrounding sea animals that keeps them warm in cold water

**WHISKERS:** On its snout. Used to detect food on bottom of ocean.

**TUSKS:** Weigh over ten pounds and are up to three feet long

**LIPS & TONGUE:** Used to suck meat out of shells

**MOUTH:** Mostly eats clams, about 4,000 in one day

Walruses in the Pacific Ocean migrate with the movement of the ice. The ice shrinks in the summer and gets larger in winter. Walruses travel by swimming around ice floes.

**Word Wise**

ICE FLOE: A sheet of floating sea ice

When at sea or on ice floes, walruses stay in small groups. They form large groups when resting on land. There can be tens of thousands of walruses packed tightly together.

Pacific walruses live in the Bering and Chukchi (sounds like CHOOK-chee) Seas and on Wrangel Island. As the ice expands in winter, they move south into the Bering Sea. As the ice shrinks in the summer, females and their young move north with the ice into the Chukchi Sea. Males often don't travel as far north. Some stay on land south of the Chukchi Sea.

Kolyma
Bay

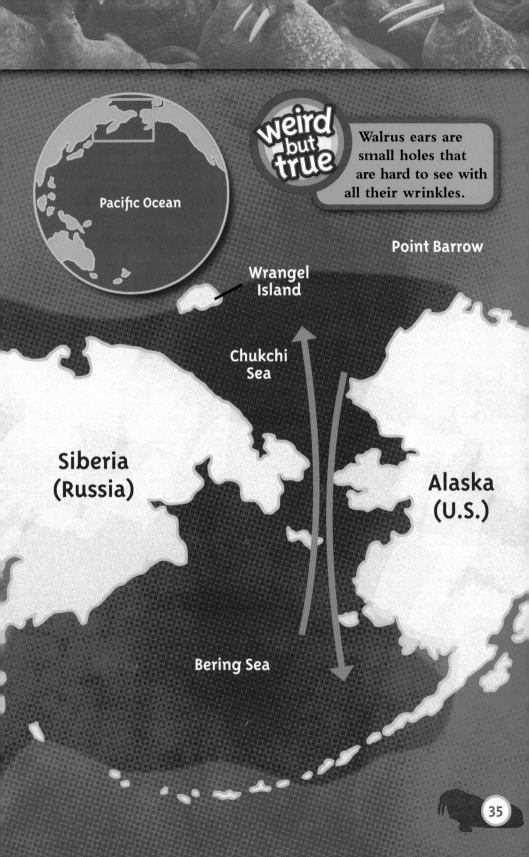

Pacific Ocean

weird
but
true

Walrus ears are
small holes that
are hard to see with
all their wrinkles.

Point Barrow

Wrangel
Island

Chukchi
Sea

Siberia
(Russia)

Alaska
(U.S.)

Bering Sea

Baby walruses are born on ice floes during the migration north. They are called calves. At birth, calves are four and a half feet long and weigh up to 150 pounds! That's as much as two large adult dogs.

weird **but** true

Walruses can break through eight inches of ice by banging it with their heads.

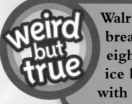

Walruses are not picky. Though they mostly eat clams, they also eat more than 60 other species of sea life. Their food includes corals, worms, shellfish, sea cucumbers, and sometimes seals.

clams

sea cucumber

lobster

**Word Wise**

SPECIES: A group of animals similar in kind

Walruses fish in waters less than 300 feet deep. They find most of their food on the bottom of the ocean. They "haul out" and rest from feeding and swimming by pulling themselves onto ice floes.

## Mighty Tusks

A walrus uses its tusks to move on land, make ice holes, and haul out of the water. Tusks are also used as protection against predators such as polar bears.

# Walruses in Trouble

As average temperatures on the Earth get warmer, walruses are losing their habitat.

Arctic summer sea ice is shrinking from the Chukchi Sea. Female walruses and their young can't move too far north with the ice because the waters there are too deep for feeding. But if they don't move with the ice, there is little land to haul out and rest. This could cause walruses to drown.

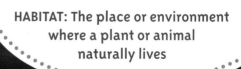

**Word Wise**

HABITAT: The place or environment where a plant or animal naturally lives

41

# Lending a Hand

Many people are working to help animals in their migration.

The zebras of Botswana have more water since people put up the fence around the national park. The paths and tunnels made for red crabs protect them on their journey to the sea.

weird but true

Walruses usually swim 4 miles an hour, but if startled, they can swim up to 22.

But there is no solution yet for the
Pacific walruses. Can you think of
ways to help them?

One way we can help is to take good care of our environment.

We can keep our oceans and rivers clean by not polluting. We can recycle so there is less trash on our Earth. We can use less energy by turning off lights when we don't need them. And we can ride bikes or take public buses or trains instead of using more gas by driving.

We can encourage others to help, too. If we all do a little, we can make a big difference.

# Glossary

**MATE:** Either a male or female in a pair. Most animals need a mate to have babies.

**CAMOUFLAGE:** An animal's natural color or form that allows it to blend in with its surroundings

**SCAVENGER:** An animal that feeds on dead plants or items left behind by others

**SPECIES:** A group of animals similar in kind

**ICE FLOE:** A sheet of floating ice

**MIGRATION:** Moving from one region or habitat to another for food or a mate

**PREDATOR:** An animal that eats other animals

**INSTINCT:** Behavior that animals are born knowing how to do

**LARVAE:** An animal's wormlike form that hatches from an egg

**BLUBBER:** Fat surrounding sea animals that keeps them warm in cold temperatures

**HABITAT:** The place or environment where a plant or animal naturally lives

47

# Index